The Actifry Cookbook

Over 70 recipes for your Actifry, Dry-fryer or Airfryer

First published December 2011

(Updated June 2013)

To Andrew

Always

Contents

Introduction

The Actifry is much more than a low fat chip fryer. It will revolutionise your cooking! Just imagine being able to simply put your food into it and walk away and use very little oil for crispy food?

Sausages will cook perfectly in about 25 minutes - no turning, no spitting, no mess on the grill - the fat accumulates in the bottom and you can just tip it away. Just One tablespoon of olive oil or less over your uncooked chips, switch it on, walk away and come back 40 minutes later to perfectly cooked chips every time.

You can brown your minced beef, cook meatballs, roast your vegetables without basting turning or even watching the clock?

You just don't need to watch it - the Actifry does all these things on automatic while you get on with other jobs. It's like having a kitchen assistant stirring the pot for you.

So how does it work?

It works with a combination of convection heat from the unit in the lid and a paddle which stirs the contents around, coating them in a thin layer of oil and allowing everything to have its share of the cooking heat

How to clean it?

The best thing about the Actifry is that the base, stirrer and lid all go in the dishwasher. And as most of the oil is absorbed but you only put a teaspoon in anyway so there isn't much to be left.

Handy Hints

- Don't add salt to chips while the chips are in the pan. Only add salt once the chips are removed from the appliance at the end of cooking.

- When adding dried herbs and spices to Actifry, mix them with some oil or liquid. If you try sprinkling them directly into the pan they will just get blown around by the hot air system.

- For best results, use finely chopped garlic instead of crushed garlic to avoid it sticking to the central paddle.

- Strong coloured spices may slightly stain the paddle and parts of the appliance.

- With meat and poultry dishes, stop the appliance and stir the pan once or twice during cooking so that the food on top does not dry out and the dish thickens evenly.

- Prepare vegetables in small pieces or stir fry size to ensure they cook through.

Cooking Guide

Potatoes

	Type	Qty	Oil	Time
Chips	Fresh	1000g (unpeeled)	1 tbs oil	40-45 mins
	Fresh	750g	½ spoonful oil	35-37 mins
	Fresh	500g	½ spoonful oil	28-30 mins
	Fresh	250g	½ spoonful oil	24-26 mins
Potatoes (quartered)	Fresh	1000g	1 tbs oil	40-42 mins
Diced	Fresh	1000g	1 tbs oil	40-42 mins
Chips	Frozen	750g	None	35-40 mins

Meat

	Type	Qty	Oil	Time
Chicken	Fresh	750g	None	10-15 mins
Lamb/Pork Chops	Fresh	2-6	None	20-25 mins
Sausages	Fresh	4-8	None	10-12 mins
Beef steak	Fresh	600g	None	8-10 mins

Fish

	Type	Qty	Oil	Time
Cod Haddock	Fresh	500g	1 sp	20-22 mins
King Prawns	Frozen or fresh	300g	None	12-14 mins

RECIPES

STARTERS

Stuck on you Chicken Wings

Ingredients

35 g flour
30 g cornstarch

1 large egg
1 tsp salt
½ tsp ground red chilli pepper
10 chicken wings,
1 tablespoon frying oil

125 ml water
(7 cm) ginger, sliced

1 ½ tbsp soy sauce
160 g dark brown sugar

1 clove garlic
3 tbs rice vinegar
160 g light corn syrup or rice syrup

35 g roasted peanuts, very coarsely chopped
2 tbs toasted sesame seeds
1 tsp red chilli flakes

Instructions

1. In a large bowl, mix together the flour, starch, egg, salt and ½ tsp ground chilli pepper until it's a thick paste.

2. Next add the wings and completely coat.

3. Put the coated wings in the Actifry and drizzle with the oil. Cook for 35 minutes, until they're brown and crispy.

4. In a large pot or wok, bring to a boil the water, ginger, soy sauce, brown sugar, vinegar, garlic (chopped) and corn or rice syrup. Let cook until the mixture becomes syrupy and thick, and starts to foam.

5. Take off the heat and stir in the cooked wings, peanuts, sesame seeds, and chilli flakes, until completely coated.

Spiced Prawns with Garlic

Ingredients

1 lb large raw prawns, shelled and deveined
2 tbs olive oil
2 tbs water
1 tsp Tabasco sauce
1 tsp red pepper flakes
1 tsp dried oregano
½ tsp dried parsley
½ tsp pepper
½ tsp garlic powder
½ tsp onion salt
½ tsp smoked paprika

Instructions

1. Place all the ingredients except for shrimp in a resealable plastic bag and mix well.
2. Add the shrimp and mix together making sure they are all coated in the mixture
3. Place in the fridge for at least 4 hours (overnight would be better)
4. Next remove the shrimp from the marinade and place in actifry.
5. Cook for around 8-10 minutes, or until they are pink.
6. Serve on a fresh salad with lemon wedges

Spanish Calamari

Ingredients

2 ½ lbs squid,
Garlic and parsley,
1 spoon wheat flour,
1 Actifry spoon of virgin olive oil,
Salt,

Instructions

1. Clean the squid and then season with salt and coat with flour, remembering to remove any excess flour.
2. Place the coated squid in Actifry with the garlic and parsley, along with a spoon of olive oil. Cook for around 15 minutes.
3. Serve chopped spring onions

New Potatoes & Prawns

Ingredients

800g Baby New Potatoes, unpeeled
1 tin chopped tomatoes, drained + ½ of its juice
1½ Actifry Spoonfuls Olive Oil
1 large Garlic Bulb
2 tbs fresh Parsley, chopped fine
12 Raw, peeled prawns
Salt And Black Pepper, to taste

Instructions

1. Place the potatoes into the Actifryer with the oil and cook for 20 minutes or until almost cooked through.
2. Next add the chopped garlic, parsley, tomatoes and cook for a further 10 minutes.
3. Finally add the prawns and cook for a further 5 minutes
4. Serve with a fresh green crunchy salad.

Oriental Sticky Ribs

Ingredients

1 rack of pork ribs
marinade:

1/3 tsp baking soda,

1tbs water,1/2 tsp salt,

1tsp sugar,

1tbs dark soya sauce,

1tbs cornstarch,

¼ tsp sesame seed oil,

1tbs minced garlic, from a jar

Instructions

1. First cut the ribs into single rib sections.
2. Mix together the remaining marinade ingredients in small bowl.
3. Coat the ribs in the marinate and if possible leave over night.
4. Add the ribs to the Actifryer and cook for 25-30 min. (this will depend how much meat is on them)

Citrus and Herb Scallops

Ingredients

1 ¼ lbs scallop's
1lb asparagus

¼ cup diced shallot
2 tbsp olive oil
2 tsp finely grated lemon zest
1 fresh chopped thyme
½ tsp salt
¼ tsp freshly ground black pepper
2 fresh lemon juice

Rocket salad to serve

Instructions

1. Rinse the scallops and then pat dry with paper towel.
2. Next trim the asparagus and cut diagonally into 1 inch pieces.
3. Place the shallots into the Actifry pan, drizzle with ½ spoonful of oil and cook for 3 minutes.
4. Add the thyme, lemon zest, asparagus, scallops salt and pepper.
5. Drizzle with the remaining oil and cook for 9 minutes, until the scallops are opaque and the asparagus is tender.
6. Drizzle with the lemon juice & serve on a bed of rocket salad

Scallops with Chips

Ingredients

1 lb sweet potatoes, ¾ -inch cubes
1 onion, ¾ -inch cubes
120ml cup soy sauce
3 tbs brown sugar
Juice of 2 limes
2 tbs canola oil
1 lb scallops
2 tbs chopped chives
canola oil, for cooking
Salt and freshly ground black pepper

Instructions

1. Combine sweet potatoes and onion and season with salt and pepper.
2. Add 1 tablespoon oil to the actifry and cook until potatoes are cooked through, (usually about 45- 50 minutes).
3. Season with salt and pepper.
4. Meanwhile, in a medium pan, add the soy sauce, brown sugar, and lime juice and reduce.
5. Transfer to a blender and blend on high speed, drizzling in oil.
6. Wash out pan and dry. On high heat, coat lightly with oil, season scallops and sear on both sides, 4 minutes total.
7. Place sweet potato and onion mixture on the plate, surround with scallops, and drizzle with syrup and garnish with chives.

Goats Cheese & Sun-dried Tomato Pastry

Ingredients

  4 oz goat cheese

  4 pieces sun-dried tomato

  7 to 10 rocket leaves

  1 sheet filo pastry

Instructions

1. Cut the filo pastry into 4 strips.
2. Place a ¼ of the fresh goat cheese on the end of each one.
3. Garnish the strips with a piece of sun-dried tomato.
4. Then add a few basil leaves on top of each pastry strip and fold up into samosas.
5. Make sure to tuck in the end of the pastry strip under the opposite layer to keep it from opening up when it cooks.
6. Place the Samosas in the Actifry and cook for 10 minutes.
7. Serve on a bed of rocket.

MAIN COURSES

Tomato and Pepper Chicken

Ingredients

500g of salad potatoes

1 tablespoon of olive oil

2 chicken breast fillets

A green and red pepper

1 tin of tomatoes

1 tsp of dried basil

Instructions

1. Take 500g of salad potatoes and cut them into small chunks.
2. Put them in the Actifry, with 1 tablespoon of olive oil and cook for around 20 minutes.
3. Chop two chicken breast fillets into medium size chunks.
4. Add them to the Actifry and cook for 5 minutes – (just enough to brown them).
5. Chop a green and red pepper into chunks – (remember to de-seed them first). Add and cook for around 5 minutes.
6. Add a tin of chopped tomatoes, stir and add a tsp of dried basil.
7. Serve with a green salad

Spring Lamb Chops

Ingredients

2 Onions

4 Large Lamb chops

2 servings of frozen vegetables (not broccoli)

Instructions

1. Heat up the Actifry for 5 minutes, and then cut up an onion into slices about 2mm thick add them.
2. After about a minute add the 4 large Lamb chops.
3. Cook for 25 minutes..
4. After 15 minutes add another cut up onion.
5. When the Actifry has finished, add 2 servings of frozen vegetables and set it to cook for a further 3 minutes.
6. Serve with brown rice & green vegetables

Chicken & Tomato Curry

Ingredients

1tsp cumin, chilli powder, garlic, ginger, ground coriander, black onion seeds, mustard seeds

1 pepper chopped

Handful of mushrooms sliced

2 tomatoes chopped

2 tsp Balti paste

2 chicken breasts (cubed)

Instructions

1. Just add the onion with very little oil, then add spices to your taste
2. Let that cook for a minute or two then add in vegetables
3. Add 2 tsp of curry paste and 150ml of water,
4. Add the breast cubes and mix with sauce.
5. Leave to cook until the chicken is done (about 10 minutes)
6. Serve with basmati rice & naan breads

Light Chicken Tikka Massala

Ingredients

500g boneless chicken cut into 2cm pieces

100g Tikka Masala curry paste.

300g low fat yogurt

1 Actifry spoon vegetable oil

1 large onion finely chopped

can of chopped tomatoes

150 ml water

1 tsp lemon

Bunch of chopped coriander.

Instructions

1. In a large bowl mix the tikka paste and yogurt.
2. Add chicken and marinate for at least two hours, or overnight if time allows.
3. Heat the oil in the Actifry for 2 minutes, add the onion and cook for 5 minutes.
4. Next add the chicken and cook for 10 minutes.
5. Add the tomatoes and water stir well and cook for a further 10 minutes
6. Add the yogurt and lemon, and stir well and cook for 5 minutes.
7. Serve with the chopped coriander and rice or naan bread.

Portuguese fish with peppers

Ingredients

1 1/3 lb white fish (cod haddock etc)
3 cloves garlic
1/2 green pepper
1 chilli pepper
1 small glass of white wine (3 1/2 fl oz)
1 tbsp olive oil
Salt to taste

Instructions

1. Wash and trim the fish and season with salt.
2. Peel and finely chop the garlic.
3. Place the garlic, the pepper cut into strips, the chilli pepper and the olive oil in Actifry and leave to cook for 10 minutes.
4. Add the diced fish and leave to cook for 10 minutes.
5. Add the white wine, stir and leave to cook for another 5 minutes.
6. Serve with tomato salad, boiled potatoes and garnish with coriander or chopped parsley (according to preference).

Butternut Squash & Nutmeg Risotto

Ingredients

1 tin of chicken broth
1 spoon olive oil
1 small onion, finely diced
100g Arborio rice
100g pureed butternut squash

¼ tsp salt
pinch ground nutmeg
75g freshly grated Parmesan cheese (1 ounce)

Instructions

1. Heat the chicken broth in a pan on the stove until it is hot but not boiling.
2. Place the oil and onion in the Actifry pan and cook until the onions are translucent, about 6 minutes.
3. Add the rice and 100g of hot chicken broth and cook until the water is mostly absorbed and the rice is partially cooked, 15 minutes.
4. Add 100g cup of broth, squash, salt and nutmeg cook for 5 minutes.
5. Add another 100g of broth and cook for 5 minutes more.
6. Add the remaining 100g of broth and cook for 5 minutes more, until liquid is thickened and mostly absorbed.
7. Stir in all but 1 tablespoon of the cheese and cook an additional 2 minutes.
8. Garnish with the remaining Parmesan cheese right before serving.

Spicy Chicken & Veg Stir-fry

Ingredients

400ml spicy Stir-Fry Sauce:
240ml Chicken Broth
1 Tbsp Light Soy Sauce

3 Tbsp Cornstarch
1 tsp sweetner

Stir Fry:

100g Broccoli
100g Snow Peas
1 large White Onion, cut into
6 pieces, then rings separated
100g Celery, sliced
1 Actifry spoonfuls Olive Oil,
1 medium Sweet Red Pepper,
Halved, sliced thin

4 ozs. Small Mushrooms,
whole halved
8 ozs. Bean Sprouts
1 lb Boneless, Skinless
Chicken Breasts, cut into bite-
size pieces
1 Actifry spoonfuls Olive Oil

Instructions

1. Combine chicken broth, soy sauce, cornstarch, and agave nectar in a small saucepan. Mix thoroughly until thickened.
2. Add broccoli, snow peas, onion, and celery to Actifryer.
3. Add 1 Actifry spoonful olive oil and cook for about 6 minutes.
4. Add red pepper and mushrooms. Cook an additional 4-5 minutes, or only until vegetables are crisp-tender. Remove all vegetables and set aside.
5. Add cut-up chicken and 1 Actifryer spoonful olive oil to Actifryer.
6. Cook until chicken is lightly browned & no longer pink. Add vegetables back to Actifryer with the chicken. Add bean sprouts; cook for 3-4 minutes or until all is hot.
7. Place in serving bowl; pour stir-fry sauce over and toss lightly.

Beef & Herb Chilli

Ingredients

1 small onion, chopped
1 medium red pepper, chopped
1 Actifry spoon olive oil
1 lb of lean ground beef
2 tsp ground cumin
1 tsp ground coriander
1 28-ounce can of fire-roasted crushed tomatoes
120ml water
2 tsp chilli powder
½ tsp dried oregano
One 15.5 ounce can of black beans, preferably low sodium
Salt and freshly ground pepper, to taste

Instructions

1. Place the onion and pepper in the Actifry pan, drizzle with oil and cook for 6 minutes.
2. Crumble the beef into the Actifry pan. Add the cumin and coriander and chilli powder cook for 5 minutes, until the meat is browned.
3. Break up any large pieces of browned meat with a wooden spoon.
4. Add the tomatoes, 60ml of the water, and oregano and cook for 25 minutes.
5. Add the beans and the remaining water and cook for 10 minutes more.
6. Season with salt and pepper to taste.

Coronation Chicken

Ingredients

1 diced large chicken breast.
3 tsp of medium curry powder
3 tbs of mayonnaise
2 tbs of peas (frozen is fine)
75g of apricots that have been soaked in 75mls of boiling water.
35g of whole almonds

Instructions

1. Add the almonds to the Actifry and cook for 5 minutes.
2. Add the chicken to the almonds and allow to cook for a further 2 minutes.
3. Mix the apricots (with the hot water), mayonnaise and curry powder together and add to the Actifry.
4. Cook for at least 10 minutes and then test some meat to ensure it is cooked thoroughly.
5. Add the peas and cook for a further 2 minutes.

Chinese Pork & Cabbage

Ingredients

1 1/3 lb pork loin, cut into thin strips
5 oz green cabbage
3 oz fresh bean sprouts,
1 oz dried black Chinese mushrooms, soaked in warm water,
1 onion,
4 cloves garlic,
2 Actifry spoons dark soy sauce,
1 Actifry spoon groundnut oil,
1 Actifry spoon dry white wine,
Salt, pepper

Instructions

1. Season the pork strips with salt and pepper. Slice the onion and the soaked mushrooms. Remove the white stalks from the cabbage leaves and cut them in half lengthwise, then slice the leaves thinly. Set aside.
2. Heat the peanut oil. Add the pork. Press 4 garlic cloves through a garlic press and put on top of the meat. Cook for 8 minutes.
3. Add the soy sauce, white wine, onion and mushrooms. Allow to reduce for 8 minutes. Add the white cabbage. Cook for 2 to 3 minutes.
4. Add the sliced green cabbage leaves and the fresh bean sprouts. Cook for 4 minutes.
5. Stop the Actifry and leave to cool for 2 minutes before serving

Hot Honey Chicken

Ingredients

500g Chicken Breast
Dried Chilli Flakes (good Pinch)
3 cloves garlic
Sea salt
Black pepper
220g runny honey
Fresh green salad
Fresh crusty bread or Rice

Instructions

1. Chop chicken into pieces (about 2inches) and put in Actifry with 1 spoon of oil
2. When Chicken starting to brown, add garlic, dried chilli's, honey, salt and pepper.
3. Cook until Chicken cooked through.
4. Serve with a fresh green salad and crusty bread, or rice, or both if you want to!

Pasta and Cheese

Ingredients

240g uncooked macaroni
180ml milk,
150g grated cheddar cheese
50g pureed winter squash, thawed if frozen
2 tbs grated Parmesan cheese
½ tsp salt
¼ tsp dry mustard

Instructions

1. Cook the macaroni according to the package directions and then drain.
2. Place ½ of milk, cheddar cheese, squash, Parmesan cheese, salt and the dry mustard into the Actifry pan and stir with a wooden spoon to combine.
3. Cook for five minutes, until the mixture is hot and the cheese is melted.
4. Add the cooked macaroni and cook two minutes more.
5. Add the remainder of the milk and cook for another two minutes.

Coconut Chicken Curry

Ingredients

1 large chicken breast
1 medium sized onion chopped
1 crushed garlic clove
1 tablespoon of olive oil, or groundnut oil
1 tsp of cumin
1 tsp of turmeric
2 tomatoes, peeled and chopped
2 tbs of desiccated coconut
1 tablespoon of ground coriander
1-2 tsps of mild curry powder (according to taste)
300mls of chicken stock.

Instructions

1. Add the diced chicken and half of the olive oil to the Actifry.
2. Cook for 5 minutes.
3. Add the chopped onion and crushed garlic to the chicken and continue to cook for a further 5 minutes.
4. Mix the spices and coconut with the remaining olive oil and add to the chicken mixture.
5. Allow to cook for 10 minutes
6. Add the tomatoes, chicken stock and cook for a further 5 - 10 minutes.
7. Add additional boiling water if the curry is too thick.

Turkey, Spring Onion & Ginger

Ingredients

4 tbsp sesame oil
700g/1lb 9oz diced turkey breast
2 bunches spring onions, trimmed and sliced on the diagonal
50g/2oz ginger root, peeled and cut into thin julienne strips
4 tbsp light soy sauce
Fresh coriander sprigs to garnish

Instructions

1. Heat the sesame oil Add the turkey for about 5 minutes until lightly browned and cooked through.
2. Add the spring onions, ginger and soy sauce. Continue to stir-fry for a further 30 seconds.
3. Serve immediately with rice and garnish with sprigs of coriander.

Mixed Vegetable Hash

Ingredients

1 chopped red onion.
1 diced red pepper
1 chopped courgette (in large chunks)
1 diced yellow pepper
Small handful of mange tout or green beans
A quarter of butternut squash, chopped small
1 carrot, chopped small
2 whole garlic cloves
2 tbs of olive oil
1 tsp of tomato puree

Instructions

1. Add the onion, peppers, butternut squash, carrot and oil to the Actifry and cook for 5 minutes.
2. Add the tomato puree, whole garlic cloves, green beans or mange tout and courgette and cook for a further 10 minutes.
3. If the mixture is sticking together add a drop of boiling water.
4. Cook for a further 10 minutes until the vegetables are tender (but still with a bit of bite to them!)
5. Allow to stand for 5 minutes before seasoning with lots of black pepper and some salt.

Cheating Chicken Fajitas

Ingredients

1 packet of Old El Paso Fajitas powder
Onions
Peppers
4 chicken breast diced

Instructions

1. Slice the peppers and onions and put in Actifry with small amount of oil cook for 5-10 mins
2. Whilst meat still wet sprinkle with spice mix so it sticks
3. Add meat to actifry and cook for 15-20 mins depending on type and thickness of meat
4. Stir with wooden spoon occasionally
5. Make sure meat is thoroughly cooked

Spicy Almond Chicken

Ingredients

4 small Chicken breasts cut crosswise into strips about 1 cm thick

½ Actifry spoon ground Coriander

60g whole raw Almonds

1 Actifry spoon Oil

1 medium Onion, rings

2 small Sweet Peppers sliced about 3mm thick

1 Carrot, cut into slices 3mm

1 stick of Celery, sliced 3mm

1 small Courgette sliced 3mm thick

2 Cloves of Garlic, minced

½ spoon Oil

½ spoon Five Spice Powder

1 hot Pepper (e.g. Jalapeno), minced finely, or ¼ tsp Cayenne pepper

200ml Chicken Stock, Juice of one Lemon

Instructions

1. Actifry spoon Cornflour, mixed in a small bowl cold water
2. Sprinkle the Coriander over the chicken breast and season with salt. Cover and refrigerate for about 30 mins
3. Put the raw Almonds in the Actifry with 1 spoon of oil and cook for 10 mins, or until golden brown and crunchy. Remove and set aside to cool
4. Put all of the vegetables (Onion, Peppers, Courgette, Carrot, Celery, Garlic) into the Actifry with half spoon of oil. Add the spice powder, hot Pepper and half of the Chicken stock. Season with a little salt if desired and cook for 20 mins.
5. Add the remaining Chicken stock, the seasoned Chicken breast strips, Lime juice and sprinkle the dissolved cornflour over the top of everything. Cook for 10 mins, or until the chicken is cooked through

Nutty Chicken Curry

Ingredients

1 kg chicken tenderloins
1 spoon oil
75g red curry paste
400ml can light coconut milk
60ml fish sauce
2 spoons sugar
1/2 cup lite crunchy peanut butter

Instructions

1. Heat oil in Actifry for around 3 minutes.
2. Cube the chicken and place into the Actifry cooking for 5 minutes.
3. Add the 60ml red curry paste cooking for a further 5 minutes.
4. Meanwhile combine coconut milk, fish sauce, sugar and peanut butter then add and cook for a further 15 minutes.
5. Serve with boiled rice.

Simple Ratatouille

Ingredients

1 onion,
2 large ripe tomatoes,
1 eggplant (Aubergine) ,
1 Courgette
2 green peppers,
1 red pepper,
2 cloves garlic,
1 Actifry spoon virgin olive oil,
Salt

Instructions

1. Dip the tomatoes in boiling water for a few seconds and then remove the skin and cut into cubes. Peel the eggplant and courgette
2. Cut all the remaining ingredients (zucchini, eggplant, peppers, garlic) in small pieces.
3. Add the oil to the Actifry pan and heat for 1 minute. First cook the onion for 7 minutes, and then add the peppers, eggplant and courgette, ending with the tomatoes, for a total of 30 minutes.
4. Set aside for about half an hour before serving.
5. Season and add a little sugar if needed, since tomatoes can be a little acidic.

Garlic & Tomato Scallops

Ingredients

240g. dry linguini, cooked
1 lb scallops, or shrimp
60g flour
4 Tbsp butter, melted
2 cloves garlic, minced
140g diced fresh tomatoes, peeled & diced
30g fresh parsley, minced
1 Tbsp lemon juice, fresh
Salt and Pepper

Instructions

1. Cook the linguini first as the scallops will cook really quickly.
2. Cut scallops in half horizontally. Dry on paper towels, then dust lightly with flour
3. Place scallops and garlic in Actifry. Pour melted butter over top.
4. Cook just until scallops are lightly brown.
5. Stir in the tomatoes, parsley, and lemon juice; cook only until heated through.
6. Season with salt and pepper to taste.
7. Serve over linguini with a fresh green salad

Pork Risotto

Ingredients

30g smoked bacon
30g diced cooked ham
210g sliced veal fillet
1 pinch saffron
100g peeled tomatoes
420ml low-fat chicken stock
100g raw Arborio risotto rice
1 clove garlic and finely chopped thyme
45g finely chopped onions
salt & pepper

Instructions

1. Brown the diced bacon in its own fat for 5 minutes in the Actifry. Remove them as soon as they begin to brown.ook the onions until soft in the bacon fat, then add the rice and cook for 2 minutes.
2. Cut the tomatoes into small dices and add together with the garlic in the Actifry.
3. Pour in the chicken stock and add the thyme and saffron. Mix and cook for 15 minutes.
4. When the rice begins to increase in volume, add the veal, ham and the bacon. Stir, adjust the seasoning and cook for about 10 additional minutes.
5. Leave to stand for 3 minutes before serving.

Mushroom & Herby Chicken

Ingredients

2 boneless chicken breasts, skinned & diced
125g sliced mushrooms

300ml chicken stock
1 sprig fresh tarragon, finely chopped
100ml Quark
50g red onion, sliced thinly
1 tbs of oil
Salt & pepper

Instructions

1. Chop the chicken breast into small bite size pieces
2. Season with salt and pepper and some of the finely chopped tarragon
3. Add the chicken pieces to the actifry and cook for about 2-3 minutes
4. Next add the red onion & mushrooms and cook for another 7 minutes.
5. Finally add the chicken stock mixed with the quark.
6. Cook for another 2-3 minutes & add finally add the chopped tarragon.

Spicy Root Vegetable Medley

Ingredients

1 kg mixed root vegetables (such as potatoes, sweet
potatoes, parsnips and swede)
2 cloves garlic, finely chopped
1 tsp hot chilli powder
1 tsp ground cumin
1 tsp ground coriander
3 spoon light olive oil
3 spoon sunflower or pumpkin seeds (optional)
Salt and freshly ground black pepper, to taste
1-2 spoon chopped fresh coriander

Instructions

1. Peel the vegetables, and then cut them into 1 cm (1/2 in) cubes.
2. Rinse the diced vegetables thoroughly, drain, then dry them well.
3. Place the vegetables in a large bowl and add the garlic and ground spices and toss together to mix well, then add 2 spoonfuls of the oil and toss together until the vegetables are coated all over.
4. Place the vegetables in the Actifry and drizzle the remaining oil over the vegetables. Cook for 20 minutes.
5. Add the sunflower or pumpkin seeds, if using, and cook for a further 5-10 minutes, or until the vegetables are tender.
6. Season to taste with salt and pepper, then stir in the chopped coriander.
7. Serve with grilled lean red meat, chicken or fish and cooked vegetables such as broccoli florets or green beans

Sweet & Sour Pork

Ingredients

1 spoon cornflour, plus extra to coat the pork strips
4 spoon red wine
300 ml (1/2 pint) passata
150 ml (1/4 pint) unsweetened apple juice
2 spoon red wine vinegar
2 spoon brown sugar

1 spoon tomato puree
600 g (1 lb 5 oz) pork fillet or pork tenderloin, cut into strips
2 onions, thinly sliced
2 spoon light olive oil
2 cloves garlic, finely chopped (optional)

Instructions

1. In a jug or bowl, blend the cornflour with the red wine until smooth, then stir in the passata, apple juice, vinegar, sugar, tomato puree and seasoning, mixing well.
2. Set aside. In a large bowl, lightly coat the strips of pork with additional cornflour. Set aside.
3. Place the onions in the Actifry pan, then drizzle the oil evenly over the onions. Cook for 5 minutes. Add the prepared pork and garlic, if using, to the Actifry and cook for 5 minutes.
4. Stir the pork to separate the pieces, then stir in the prepared sweet and sour sauce. Cook for a further 10 minutes, or until the pork is cooked and tender and the sauce is thickened.
5. Stop the Actifry once during cooking and stir the mixture using a wooden spoon or spatula.
6. Adjust the seasoning to taste and serve with cooked rice or mashed potatoes and stir-fried spring greens or cabbage.

Salmon & Mushrooms

Ingredients

4 large Salmon Fillets

Mushrooms

1 tbsp Parsley

Instructions

1. Cut the boneless salmon fillets in half
2. Clean and chop the mushrooms into small chunks
3. Add all ingredients into the Actifryer and drizzle 1tbs of oil and cook for around 10 minutes.
4. Add tbsp of parsley
5. Season to taste and serve with rice or a green salad

Mexican Beef Taco

Ingredients

1 tbs Oil
Pre made taco shells
2 tablespoon Tomato paste
1 Onion
1 Aubergine
1 Courgette
2 peppers
2 cloves garlic
salt and pepper
500g beef mince
120g low fat cheese.

Instructions

1. Heat the oil for 1 min in the Actifryer
2. Add the mince beef and cook for 5 mins or until browned
3. Peel and remove the skin from the Aubergine, and cut into pieces along with courgette, peppers and garlic,
4. Add to the mince and add then 1 - 2 tbs of the tomato sauce/paste.
5. Cook for around 30 minutes adding salt and pepper near end.
6. Fill the taco shells, and cover with cheese on top (place in an oven to brown if desired).

Curried Salmon

Ingredients

12 30-g cubes salmon,
1/2 cucumber,
1 tsp green chilli,
½ red onion,
1 small tomato,
1 ½ Actifry spoons tandoori spice powder,
3 individual pots of plain yoghurt,
½ Actifry spoon ground cumin,
30 leaves fresh mint

Instructions

1. Trim the salmon into cubes and coat with tandoori spice powder. Chill and leave to marinate (overnight if possible)
2. Blend ¼ of the yoghurt with the chilli, mint, cumin, salt and pepper. Refrigerate.
3. Peel the tomato. Remove the seed and cut into a small chunks.
4. Peel and finely chop the onion.
5. Peel the cucumber. Cut lengthwise to remove the seeds easily using a small spoon, then dice.
6. Right before serving, cook the salmon in the Actifry for 5 to 6 minutes, adding seasoning but no fat.
7. During this time, mix the flavoured yoghurt with the remaining yoghurt, the tomato dice, the cucumber dice and the chopped onion.
8. Pour the sauce into small glasses or soup plates and top with the salmon.

9. The salmon will be half-cooked after 5 to 6 minutes. If you prefer it more cooked, continue for another 4 to 5 minutes.

Traditional Sausage and Beans

Ingredients

1 Small Diced Onion

¾ Lb Italian Sausage

1 tin Cannellini Beans

1 Clove Minced Garlic

2 Tbsp White Wine

1 Small Tomato

180ml Chicken Stock

1 tsp Italian Spices, Salt and Pepper (to taste)

1 Bunch Baby Spinach

Instructions

1. First cook onion and loose sausage for around 7 minutes in the Actifryer
2. Break up the sausage in to chunks and add ½ tsp of olive oil.
3. Dice the tomato and along with the remaining ingredients cook for 5-7 minutes.
4. Finally add a little more chicken stock if it appears too thick.
5. Serve over pasta, or with chunky bread.

Veal & Herb Stew

Ingredients

420g veal haunch, diced,
210g fresh bitter endive leaves,
1 Actifry spoon extra virgin olive oil,
210g basmati rice,

Instructions

1. Pour a spoon of extra virgin olive oil into the Actifry and heat for 1 minute. Add the veal and cook for 6 minutes until evenly browned.
2. Add the bitter endive leaves and cook for another 4 minutes.
3. Add the basmati rice, already cooked. Season with salt and cook for another 4 minutes.

Sticky Pork

Ingredients

750g Pork loin, cut into sticks
1 ½ Actifry spoons of Soy sauce
½ tablespoon of sugar
1 tbs Olive Oil

Instructions

1. Marinate the pork in a mixture of soy sauce, ½ tbs of oil and sugar for at least 1 hour.
2. Place the marinated pork in the Actifry add a ½ tbs of oil. Cook for around 15 minutes.
3. To make the Egg fried rice, boil some plain rice, drain it and add it to a frying pan with 2 beaten eggs, a handful of petit pois, 1 chopped small onion & some soy sauce. Stir fry for 5-6 minutes.
4. When the pork and rice are ready, stir until mixed together & serve.

Citrus Chilli Chicken

Ingredients

3 cubed Chicken Breasts
1 red chilli, deseeded and chopped finely
3 lemons, juice and zest
3 cloves of garlic. Finely chopped
1 onion thinly sliced small waxy salad potatoes, halved lengthways
(as many as your appetite desires)
12 cherry tomatoes, halved
2 tbs olive oil (or any kind you like)

Instructions

1. Mix together the chicken, chilli, garlic, onion, lemon juice and zest, 1 tablespoon of the oil, then leave to stand.
2. Put the potatoes in the Actifry, drizzle with 1 tablespoon of the oil, cook for 15 minutes.
3. Add the chicken mixture and cook for another 15 minutes.
4. Add the cherry tomatoes and cook for a further 5 minutes.

Breakfast Brunch

Ingredients

2 small Potatoes, peeled and cut into 1/2 inch chunks
1 Actifry spoon Olive Oil
½ small Onion, sliced into rings 1/4 inch thick
1 tsp Provencal Herbs or mixed Herbs
8 button Mushrooms, cleaned dried and quartered
1 Actifry spoon Olive Oil
60g Bacon, sliced into strips
4 thin sausages
2 medium tomatoes, cut into 1/2 inch chunks
2 eggs

Instructions

1. Wash, drain and dry the potato chunks, and place in the Actifry with one spoon of oil poured over the top. Cook for around 10 mins
2. Separate the onion into individual rings and arrange over the potatoes. Cook for another 5 mins
3. Add the herb mix and mushrooms. Sprinkle the second spoon of oil over the mixture. Add the sausages and cook 10 minutes
4. Add the bacon and cook for another 5 minutes
5. Finally add the tomatoes and cook for the final 5 mins. While the tomatoes soften, cook the eggs in a separate pan (fry for 4 mins on a low heat, covered)

Steak with Red Wine Sauce

Ingredients

400g sirloin steak
400g potatoes
1 red pepper
1 tablespoon of red wine
1 tsp of cayenne chilli pepper

Instructions

1. Cut the steak into small chunks and then marinate in the red wine, with the chilli pepper. (if possible overnight)
2. Cut the potatoes & red pepper into small pieces.
3. Put the potatoes & the peppers in the Actifry, add salt & pepper & cook for around 12 minutes
4. Next add the marinated meat, & cook for another 5 minutes (or until the meat is cooked).

Full English Breakfast

Ingredients

2 Sausages
2-3 rashes of smoked bacon cut into chunks
1 small potato cut into cubes
A few mushrooms chopped into chunks
Half a tin of baked beans
Half a tin of chopped tomatoes
1 Egg, poached or fried

Instructions

1. Cook the sausages & potatoes for 10 minutes in the Actifry.
2. Add the chopped bacon for a further 10 minutes.
3. Add the mushrooms & allow to brown for around 5 minutes.
   Add the baked beans & tomatoes.
4. Cook your egg to your liking in a pan & serve altogether.

Stuffed Cheese and Garlic Mushrooms

Ingredients:

8 Large Flat Field Mushrooms
1 tbs olive Oil
Salt and Pepper
4 Garlic Cloves
3 Large Tomatoes
170g Mozzarella Cheese
312g Baby Spinach

Instructions

1. First clean the mushrooms and remove the stalks.
2. Drizzle the oil over the mushrooms and place on a grill rack.
3. Grill gently for 5 minutes then turn them over.
4. Season with salt and pepper and grill for another 5 minutes until they start to weep. Remove them from the grill and set aside.
5. In a bowl peel and crush the garlic, cut the tomatoes into 8 slices and grate the mozzarella.
6. Add the garlic and spinach and then place on top of the mushroom.
7. Place a tomato over each mushroom and sprinkle with the cheese.
8. Place in Actifryer for 2-3 minutes or until bubbling. Serve immediately.

DESSERTS

Deep Fried Banana

Ingredients

5 large bananas

1 tbs brown sugar

Instructions

1. Slice 5 large bananas and put them into the Actifry,
2. Add 1 spoonful of brown sugar and cook for about 5 minutes
3. Ensure they stay intact and are not at all mushy.
4. Serve with vanilla ice-cream and some maple syrup.

Apple & Cinnamon

Ingredients

4 Green Eating Apples
1 spoon Sunflower Oil
3oz Ready-to-eat Dried Apricots, finely chopped
1-2 spoons Caster Sugar
½ tsp Ground Cinnamon, or to taste

Instructions

1. Peel the apples, then cut each one into quarters and remove and discard the cores and pips.
2. Cut each apple quarter in half again, to make a total of 8 even wedges.
3. Place the apple wedges in a large bowl, add the oil and toss to mix until the apples are coated all over.
4. Place the apple wedges in the Actifry and cook for 12-15 mins.
5. Add the chopped apricots and cook for a further 3 minutes.
6. In a small bowl, mix together the sugar and cinnamon.
7. Serve the hot cooked apple wedges with a sprinkling of cinnamon sugar and serve with vanilla ice cream.

Apples Surprise

Ingredients

2-3 apples,
2-3 pears,
3 1/2 cup walnuts,
225g vanilla-flavoured cream,
1 spoon oil,
1 spoon apple juice,
a pinch of ground cinnamon

Instructions

1. Peel the apples and pears and cut into wedges
2. Mix the fruit with the rapeseed oil and the cinnamon. Put in the Actifry and set the timer for 10 minutes.
3. After 5 minutes, add the walnuts and raisins.
4. Mix the cream well with the apple juice and add 2 minutes before the cooking is finished

Sweet Sugar Pear & Cream

Ingredients

4 Pears
4 tbs Brown sugar

Instructions

1. Peel and cut into small chunks pears
2. Sprinkle over with brown sugar and rub into pears
3. Put straight into Actifry and cook for 15-20 mins until tender and then finished off 3 mins before needed
4. Serve with fresh double cream or vanilla ice cream

Cherry Flapjack Crunch

Ingredients

200g oats
150g coarsely chopped, unsalted pecans
½ Actifry spoon oil
180ml maple syrup or golden syrup
½ tsp vanilla extract
¼ tsp ground cinnamon
60g dried cherries

Instructions

1. Put the oats, pecans, oil, maple syrup, vanilla and cinnamon in a large mixing bowl and stir until evenly coated.
2. Put the oat mixture into the Actifry pan and cook for 7 minutes, until the oats and nuts are well toasted.
3. Add the cherries and cook for one minute more.
4. Remove the Actifry pan from its base and allow the mixture to cool for 15 minutes. It will crisp further as it cools.

Alcoholic Fruit Compote

Ingredients

50g halved, dried apricots
50g dried cranberries or sour cherries
25g dried blueberries
240ml dessert wine or 240ml white grape juice

1 tsp finely grated orange zest.

Instructions

1. Place the apricots, cranberries, blueberries, ice wine and juice in a non-reactive bowl. Soak for 30 minutes
2. Transfer the fruit and all liquid to the Actifry pan.
3. Cook for 20 minutes or until fruit is plump and liquid is slightly thickened.
4. Stir in the orange zest. Serve warm.
5. For an alcohol-free version, replace the wine with white grape juice

Spiced Apple Crumble

Ingredients

APPLE CRUMBLE:
75g nuts (walnuts, pecans)
roughly chopped
45g all-purpose flour
50g cup rolled oats
50g cup dark brown sugar
½ tsp five-spice powder
¼ tsp salt
4 tbs melted unsalted butter

APPLE FILLING:
4 granny smith apples,
peeled, cored and chopped
into ½ -inch dice juice of ½
lemon
45g dark brown sugar,
packed
½ tsp five spice powder

Instructions

1. Make the "crumble:" In a medium bowl, combine nuts, flour, oats, brown sugar, five-spice powder and salt. Stir to combine. Add the melted butter to the bowl and mix. Add the crumble mixture to the Actifry.
2. Set the timer to 20 minutes and start the Actifry. Transfer the finished crumble to a sheet tray. Be careful as the mixture is very hot because of the caramelized sugar. Set aside to cool.
3. In a bowl, combine the diced apples, lemon juice, brown sugar and five-spice powder. Add the apple mixture to the Actifry, set the timer for 12 minutes and start the Actifry.
4. After the apples have cooked for 12 minutes, add 250g crumble mixture to the apple mixture. Allow the mixture to cook until warmed through and moist, about 3 additional minutes.
5. Serve with ice cream.

Banana & Chocolate

Ingredients

4 bananas
1 tablespoon cocoa nibs
9 sheets pastry

SAUCE :

150g chocolate (70% cocoa solids)
2 Actifry spoons milk

Instructions

1. Cut the bananas into pieces (½ -inch thick). Cut the pastry sheets into 4.
2. Put a pinch of cocoa on each pastry sheet. Top with a piece of banana. Fold over two sides first, then the other two to close the packets. Tie with a little kitchen string.
3. Put the packets in the Actifry and cook for 10 minutes.
4. During this time, heat the milk in a seperate pan.
5. In a seperate bowl pour it over the chocolate and blend until you have a smooth sauce.
6. Pour over the banana pastries.

Mixed Berry Stew

Ingredients

500g unsweetened frozen mixed berries

3 tbsp sugar, plus more to taste
2 tbsp orange liqueur
2 lemon juice
1 tbsp cornstarch, dissolved in 3 tbs cold water

Instructions

1. Put the berries, 3 tbs of sugar, orange liqueur, lemon juice and dissolved cornstarch into the Actifry pan and cook until the liquid has thickened and the fruit has softened, (usually 20 minutes).
2. Taste and add more sugar to taste if necessary.
3. Allow to cool slightly before serving or serve at room temperature.

Cinnamon Pears

Ingredients

4 ripe pears
2 tbs of good quality oil
85g (3 ounces) of sultanas or raisins.
2 tbs of brown sugar
Half a tsp of ground cinnamon.
Drizzle of honey

Instructions

1. Peel the pears and chop into quarters.
2. Remove all the core and pips.
3. Slice each quarter into two halves.
4. Add the pear chunks to the Actifry with the oil and cook for 10 minutes.
5. Add the sultanas and cook for about another 5 minutes or until the pears are almost tender.
6. Mix the sugar and cinnamon together and pour over the pears.
7. Cook for 1 minute.
8. Drizzle about a tablespoon of honey over the pears before serving.

Pineapple & Banana

Ingredients

2 sliced bananas
approx same amount of pineapple chunks
1 spoon melted butter
1-2 spoons of honey
Vanilla ice cream

Instructions

1. Add the bananas and pineapple, butter, and honey to the Actifry
2. Cook for around 15 minutes.
3. Serve and allow to cool then add vanilla ice cream

Mixed Berry Delight

Ingredients

450g of mixed red fruits
½ tbsp of extra virgin olive oil
75g of brown sugar
200mls of apple juice
100g of marshmallows

Instructions

1. Place all the red fruit into the Actifry and add the oil.
2. Cook for 5 minutes.
3. Add half of the apple juice and the sugar and continue to cook for a further 5 minutes.
4. Stir in the marshmallows to the fruit and cook for a couple of minutes.
5. Ideally the marshmallows need to be only slightly melted.
6. If you want a runnier consistency add more of the remaining apple juice, otherwise leave as it is.
7. Pour into separate serving bowls and chill for a couple of hours.
8. Decorate with a glace cherry or sprig of mint.

Individual Fig Crumbles

Ingredients

1 3/4 lb figs (fresh or frozen)
2 oranges, zested

CRUMBLE:
50g oz rolled oats
50g cup butter
50g cup flour
50g cup sugar

Instructions

1. Mix the crumble dough together until smooth.
2. Make large balls of the dough and put them in the Actifry pan.
3. Cook for 20 to 25 minutes. Set aside.
4. Place the frozen figs into the Actifry and cook for 10 minutes.
5. Zest the oranges, then peel and separate into wedges. Add the orange wedges and the zest to the figs and cook for another 5 minutes.
6. Divide the fruit among 6 ramekins and cover with the crumble dough.
7. Serve with vanilla icecream

Pineapple & Figs Dipped in Honey

Ingredients

1 pineapple
4 fresh figs
1 tbsp lemon juice
3 tbsp honey
1 pinch of ground cinnamon

Instructions

1. Cut off the crown and the lower part of the pineapple. Cut it into eight lengthways. Remove the core and the skin and chop the flesh into cubes.
2. Place the pineapple pieces in the Actifry, pour in two tbs of honey and cook for 10 minutes.
3. Meanwhile wash the figs and cut them into quarters.
4. Add the figs with the remaining tablespoon of honey, the lemon juice and the cinnamon. Cook for 4 to 5 minutes.
5. Serve the pineapple and figs with vanilla ice cream.

Nutella & Cinnamon Sweet Crisps

Ingredients

Plain unsalted Tortillas, 1 per person (up to 6, minimum 2,)
Oil, 1 tbsp per tortilla
Cinnamon to taste
Caster Sugar to taste
Nutella and whipped cream to serve

Instructions

1. Cut the tortillas into chips and place in the Actifry.
2. Mix the Oil and Cinnamon and add to the Actifry.
3. Cook for around 10 minutes, until the cinnamon mix completely covers the tortilla chips.
4. Remove from the Actifry and place in a container/bag with the sugar, seal and shake to coat.
5. Put the chips in a bowl and serve with the dips (Nutella and whipped cream)

SIDE DISHES

Roasted Vegetables

Ingredients

100g Carrots

100g parsnips

250g potatoes

1 red pepper

1 tbs oil

Instructions

1. Peel and cut your veg into even sized chunks
2. Put in the potatoes, sprinkle about a tablespoon of oil over, then switch on and time for 10 minutes.
3. Add carrots, cook for 10 minutes.
4. Add parsnips and peppers and cook for a further 20 minutes.
5. Serve as an accompaniment to a main meal

Curried Cauliflower

Ingredients

1 large cauliflower, divided into florets,
3 apples, diced,
4 spoons raisins,
½ tsp curry powder,
1 tsp chopped fresh dill,
Salt and freshly ground pepper,
1 tsp oil of your choice

Instructions

1. Wash the cauliflower and divide up into florets and dice the apples.
2. Pour a small spoonful of oil in the Actifry pan.
3. First add the curry. When it begins to smell good, add the cauliflower, apples, raisins and salt.
4. Add a good pinch of freshly ground pepper and simmer for 20 minutes.
5. Add the dill at the last minute.

Bacon, Leeks & New Potatoes

Ingredients

200g salad potatoes diced

1/2 sliced leek and

60g chopped lean bacon

½ tsp paprika

Handful of baby spinach

Instructions

1. Cook the diced potatoes in 1tsp oil n the Actifry.
2. Add the sliced leek and cook for a few more minutes
3. Then add the chopped lean bacon
4. Next sprinkle in about ½ tsp of smoked paprika
5. Add a handful of baby spinach and cook until the bacon is cooked through and the spinach wilted.

Sour Cream Potato Skins

Ingredients

3 Large baking potatoes
4-5 Strips of bacon
1 onion
200g Cheddar cheese
100ml Sour Cream
Veg oil

Instructions

1. Wash and cut baking potatoes in half
2. Coat the potatoes with the oil.
3. Place the potatoes (cut side up) in the Actifryer 35 to 40 mins
4. For the last 10 minutes add sliced bacon.
5. Next chop onions and grate the cheese and place to one side.
6. When the potatoes are ready, remove and scoop out the centre
7. Mix the potato with the sour cream (until moist but not runny) and the bacon strips
8. Cover with the grated cheddar cheese and put back in the fryer until browned

Simply Roasted Turnips

Ingredients

1 purple top turnip cubed about 1 inch pieces
(I prefer triangle shaped cubes so it get's all the edges)
1 tbsp olive oil or butter (yum!)
1/4 tsp. nutmeg

Instructions

1. Clean and cube the turnip into 1 inch pieces
2. Place into actifry with 1tbs of oil and salt and pepper to taste
3. Sprinkle a little nutmeg over the turnip
4. Cook for 35-40 minutes until soft

Love/Hate Chips

Ingredients

1kg of peeled potatoes.
2 tsps of marmite/vegimite
2 tbs of sesame seeds.
1 tablespoon of olive oil.

Instructions

1. Chop the potatoes into evenly sized chips (or wedges if preferred).
2. Wash the potatoes and dry with a tea towel.
3. Place the potatoes into the Actifry.
4. Mix the sesame seeds with the oil and add to the Actifry.
5. Cook for 10 minutes.
6. Lift the lid (which will pause the cooking process) and add marmite.
7. Allow to cook for a further 10 - 15 minutes until browned.

Roast Traditional Potatoes

Ingredients

12 Maris piper potatoes
5 cloves of garlic not peeled
virgin olive oil

Instructions

1. Peel wash and dry potatoes place in Actifry with garlic cloves
2. Drizzle with oil and cook for 40-45mins
3. Serve potatoes and garlic cloves.

European Potatoes

Ingredients

1 kg (2.2 lbs) of potatoes.
1 tbsp of oil (I use Olive Oil).
1 tsp of smoked paprika.
2 medium red onions.
125 gm (4oz) cooking chorizo.

Instructions

1. Peel the potatoes and cut into 2.5cm (1") chunks. Rinse in cold running water, drain and then dry carefully.
2. Place in the Actifry.
3. Mix the oil and paprika together and drizzle over the potatoes.
4. Switch on and leave to cook for about 45 minutes.
5. Meanwhile, peel and quarter the onions. Peel the chorizo and cut into 10mm (3/8") cubes.
6. After 45 minutes the potatoes should be nearly cooked, but check with a skewer or fork and increase time if necessary.
7. Then add the chorizo and onions and cook for a further 10 minutes.
8. Remove from the Actifry and serve.

Herb & Garlic Breaded Mushrooms

Ingredients

1 pkt Breadcrumbs
50g Flour
Mushrooms
1 Egg
Garlic salt

Instructions

1. Wash mushrooms prepare three ramekins or bowls.
2. In the first one crack an egg, and mix in a dash of salt and pepper In the second put in some flour
   In the third mix bread crumbs with any preferred spice (parmesan and green onion, or chilli powder, Cajun seasoning, etc)
3. Dip a mushroom in flour, then egg, and then crumb mixture. Repeat until all mushrooms are done.
4. Place mushrooms in the Actifry and spoon over 1 spoon of oil, cook for 15 minutes.
5. Serve with a garlic mayonnaise dressing

Frozen Chips

Ingredients

750 g (1 lb 10 oz) frozen chips
1 spoon sunflower oil
Sea Salt, to taste

Instructions

1. Place the chips in the Actifry and drizzle the oil evenly over the chips.
2. Cook for 30-35 minutes or until the chips are cooked.
3. Serve immediately, sprinkled with crunchy salt to taste.

End

More titles by this Author

- Halogen Heaven

- Health Halogen

- Quick & Easy – Halogen Cooking for one

- 200 Halogen Oven Recipes

- The 5:2 Diet Cookbook

- The Modern Slow cooker Cookbook

Visit www.Amazon.co.uk to find out more...

DISCLAIMER
IMPORTANT -- PLEASE READ

This publication is an informational product based on the authors own experience and research. It is not affiliated with Actifry or any other Airfryer manufacturer. It has not been evaluated by any medical professional. The Author and Publisher assume no responsibility or liability whatsoever on the behalf of any purchaser or reader of these materials. The author is not a professional chef, nor does she claim to be.

As always, before attempting anything mentioned in this book, or if you are in doubt, you should use your best judgment. If you fail to do so, you are acting at your own risk. You, the buyer or reader of this book, alone assume all risk for anything you may learn from this book.

By choosing to use the information made available in this book, you agree to indemnify, defend, and hold harmless the author of this book from all claims (whether valid or invalid), suits, judgment, proceedings, losses, damages, costs and expenses, of any nature whatsoever (including reasonable fees) for which the author of this book may become liable resulting from the use or misuse of any products sold.

7346568R00050

Printed in Great Britain
by Amazon.co.uk, Ltd.,
Marston Gate.